THE GREAT GODDESS

An Introduction to Her Many Names

Martha Ann • Dorothy Imel • Lee Redfield • Barbara J. Suter

Edited by Mary K. Headley

Cover illustration: *The Goddess Has A Thousand Faces*
mandala by Lydia Ruyle
collagraph collage — 54″ x 54″ x 2″—1987

For more copies or information, contact:

Our Many Names
c/o Lee Redfield
137 31st Street
Boulder, CO 80303-3401

ISBN #0-9638567-0-7

PREFACE

The goal of the women who collaborated on this booklet is to empower you as a woman. As a girl, you may have been taught that goddesses were confined to the classical Greek and Roman period. However, we now know that female deities have been present for thousands of years, in nearly every part of the world. By letting you sample from the richness of female deity worship throughout "her-story," we hope you can gain new recognition of your own special powers.

Of the many geographical/cultural areas with a bountiful goddess tradition, this booklet covers nine: Africa, Egypt, Greece, India, Japan, Mesoamerica, Mesopotamia, North America, and Semitic-speaking peoples. (We chose to describe Egypt separately from Africa and the Semitic culture separately from Mesopotamia because of their unique goddess heritages.) Each chapter covers one of these areas and is organized into the following sections:

- Martha Ann gives you an historical overview, covering early evidence of goddess worship, popular goddess traditions, effects of patriarchal religion, and current feminist thought. (Notes and key references are listed in the Readings section at the end of each chapter.)

- Dottie Imel introduces you to individual deities with a cross-section of the more prominent goddesses worshiped. These were selected from our data base of over 11,000 goddess descriptions.

- Lee Redfield elaborates on a particular goddess story, providing a modern slant for reclaiming power that might apply to your life. Stories were chosen to exemplify a variety of goddess-like personality characteristics present in many women.

- B.J. Suter illustrates each of these stories for your visual enjoyment.

Mary Headley edited and helped design the booklet, and Lydia Ruyle created the composite goddess picture shown on the cover.

At the end of the booklet, we list further readings so that you can continue your explorations. We also invite you to read the fuller spectrum of goddess stories contained in our reference dictionary, *Goddesses in World Mythology*.

It is our hope that, after this brief introduction to 30,000 years of goddess worship, you will be encouraged to continue learning and dreaming, thereby enhancing your own spiritual power and finding creative expression for that power in your life.

CONTENTS

INTRODUCTION

The Paleolithic period of gathering and hunting accounts for over 99% of human existence. From this period, dating back some 30,000 years, the earliest depictions of humans are small figurines of nude females. These figurines have been found across a wide area in Europe and the Middle East, from the Venus of Willendorf statuette in Germany made about 26,000 B.C.E. (before current era) to the Indus Valley carvings from around 1000 B.C.E. "Some people believe that a goddess of fertility or a Mother Goddess is represented, while others have suggested that the figurines are part of sympathetic magic rituals aimed at making individual women pregnant. The reader must in the end make up her or his own mind ... " (Ehrenberg, 73). Although no one can ever know exactly what life was like during these times, the authors of this book believe the archaeological evidence certainly points to the worship of a primordial goddess.

Early humans likely observed women giving birth by seemingly magical means (the male role in procreation being obscured for some time to come). It is natural, then, that early religious figures would be female—goddesses. Such powerful "magic" could surely bless the tribe, the animals, and the environment to ensure survival.

As horticultural communities developed, fertility/earth mother goddesses continued to be worshiped. It is believed that Neolithic peoples lived a life closely attuned to seasonal cycles. "In these simple villages, a new mythology was born. Centered on the female figure...this mythology...saw the earth as the repository of spirit and saw that spirit, or life force, as the source and sustainer of all life, an abiding maternal presence to which the omnipresent female figurines gave mythic form" (Markman, 7).

As Neolithic communities grew to rely on herding and agriculture, male deities—gods of war and weather—evolved. Originally the sole and universal creator, the goddess was gradually given a son or a lover, who was then added to the pantheon. At first an equal partner to these new deities, the goddess gradually was reduced in status to merely the wife, sister, or mother of these powerful and often frightening gods.

By the time agricultural advances made great cities possible, men began to dominate culturally and religiously. "Emerging civilizations rallied around these official gods, constructing for them elaborate rituals, great temples, and political priesthoods. For these new gods, war and conquest were religious imperatives." (Chambers, 6). As patriarchy became entrenched, the ancient goddesses were subdued, fragmented, co-opted, demonized, demoted to sainthood, killed, and obliterated. Gods now reigned supreme, sometimes even taking over the female role of birthing.

In addition to to the demise of the goddess, the advent of patriarchal rule led to a lower socio-economic status for women that persists today. Sometimes this lower status is merely subtle; in many parts of the world it is flagrant. According to Barber Conable, President of World Bank, "Women do two-thirds of the world's work. They produce 60 to 80% of Africa's and Asia's food, and 40% of Latin America's. Yet they earn only one-tenth of the world's income and own less than 1% of the world's property. They are among the poorest of the world's poor ... Women live terrible lives of poverty, history, tradition, religion, caste, overpopulation, and male control of their lives from before birth to the grave ... Slowly I realized that the way Indian women live is the way the majority of women in the world spend their lives; it is Americans who are peculiar" (Bumiller, 13-23).

Though attempts to extinguish the Great Goddess continue to the present time, remnants of her presence have always been kept alive through the ages. For example, the three daughters of the Islamic Allah were originally powerful goddesses, and the Japanese monarchy still pays homage to the sun goddess Amaterasu. The mighty goddess Kwannon is actively worshipped in many Buddhist areas today and Pele is still propitiated in Hawaii to protect her followers from volcanoes. The nested matrioska dolls in Russia and many of today's Virgin Mary cults harken back to indigenous goddesses.

These vestiges of the goddess are all the more remarkable since the histories of many peoples, notably Africans and Asians, were compiled by patriarchally-inclined Europeans who did not record the full account of female deities. But modern women are reaching behind patriarchy to rediscover their goddess heritage, seeking to combine the best of past and present religious traditions. The result is a powerful resurgence of the Great Goddess in women's lives today.

Bumiller, Elisabeth. *May You Be the Mother of a Hundred Sons: A Journey Among the Women of India.* New York: Fawcett Columbine, 1990.

Chambers, Marlene, editor. *Little People of the Earth: Ceramic Figures from Ancient America.* Denver: Denver Art Museum, 1990.

Ehrenberg, Margaret. *Women in Prehistory.* Norman: University of Oklahoma Press, 1989.

Markman, Roberta A. and Peter T. Markman. *The Flayed God: The Mythology of Mesoamerica.* New York: HarperCollins Publishers, 1992.

Africa

African Goddess History

While the Ice Age chilled Europe, the Sahara was a fertile region, supporting what is now believed to be the first humans. Their prolific rock art dates from as early as 7000 B.C.E. During the Herder period (1500-600 B.C.E.), beautiful scenes were carved and painted on rocks in the Inaouanrhat area that indicate women were held in great regard. The depicted women tended cattle, raised children, hunted, and gathered food; they made baskets, pottery, jewelry, and household tools. A striking example is the painting entitled the "Horned Goddess of Tassili."

Archaeological evidence and oral traditions indicate that early Africans worshiped the goddess during Paleolithic and Neolithic times (McCall, 308). Numerous large-hipped and full-breasted figurines, believed to be deities of life and fertility, have been found throughout Africa, dating back to 3000 B.C.E. (Gillon, 58) The various earth mother cults among the Akan, Yoruban, and Ibo can be seen as remnants of this Neolithic religion.

About 2000 B.C.E., when the dried Sahara became a major barrier, the history of Africa went in two directions: the people to the north of the Sahara created the famous civilization of Egypt, and those to the south dispersed into many groups, each with its own language, religion, and social order.

As complex societies in the south evolved, domination by males began. At the same time, the goddess as supreme creator became the subordinate wife, sister, or mother of the many new male gods. For example, the powerful Yoruban goddesses, Oya and Oshun, became wives of the god Shango, mere shadows of their former selves. Subsequent Arab invasions and European colonizations, with their patriarchal Islamic and Christian beliefs, added to the demise of the goddess.

African goddess-based religion came to the Americas with the slave trade, although it was changed by associations with the new cultures, by the loss of close family ties, and by the imposition of Christianity. However, its influence is still present in many areas today, notably Brazil and the Caribbean. Likewise, the goddess tradition can still be found in many African cultures: the Ashanti of Ghana; the Dahomey, Mashona and Buhera Ba Rowzi of Zimbabwe; the Sulu of Natal; and the Woyo of Zaire. To conceive and to assure the birth of a beautiful child, preferably a daughter, Ashanti women continue to wear Akua'ba, female figurines, and worship them in shrines (Gillon, 140).

Today African women, whether in Africa or in the countries where they now live, are re-birthing the image of the goddess in their lives and are finding regeneration and empowerment. "Mama" is the original word used to describe the Mother Goddess concept among African peoples. Asungi, an Afracentric ritualist, says "We, Afrikan wimmin...must re-claim our Dark Connections, our Roots...our Afra-Mama! We must continue to re-member positive images of ourselves from the past and for the future. As the Mamaroot vision grows deeper and stronger in us...we will fly!"(Asungi, 37)

African Goddesses

Ala—Ibo Divine Mother who gives life and is the custodian of her children, providing all that is life sustaining, establishing laws, guiding morality, and finally, claiming them in death. If her children are peaceful, there will be bountiful harvests from the earth and the womb. Shrines to Ala are found in Nigerian homes and village squares.

Atai—Efik goddess who encouraged the creation of humans, choosing earth for us to inhabit. When, as she feared, we independent mortals forgot our creator and attempted to become equals of the deities, Atai sent death as a potent reminder that we are only human.

Bunzi—Woyo rain goddess of Zaire. She manifests as a rainbow-colored snake and is invoked for plentiful rains and harvests.

Chineke—Ibo creator goddess of Nigeria. She protects those who are good and punishes those who are evil.

Eka Abassi—Goddess of the Ibibio people. She came before everything and created humans.

Igbarun—Nigerian river goddess who is wed to the king of the sea. As a couple, they are all earth's water.

Isamba—Moon goddess of the Issansun people of Tanzania who is married to the sun. They had a contest to see who was the wisest.

Kono—A bird goddess, Kono is the ancestor deity of the Senufu people of the Ivory Coast and Mali. She is worshiped in the form of a large crested crane.

Mawu-lisa—Dahomey supreme deity. Mawu, the moon, is the female half of this androgynous deity. She is called the wife or twin of Lisa, the sun. Together they created all the other deities. An eclipse happens when the two mate.

Minona—Protector of women of Benin who gives fertility to women and the fields. She uses palm kernels to divine the future. Every Dahoman woman has a shrine for Minona in her house where offerings of fresh fruit are made.

Nagadya and **Nagawonyi**—When there are droughts, or the gods are being difficult,

these Ugandan goddesses are asked to intercede on behalf of humans. They cause the rains to fall, allowing food to grow once more.

Nasilele—Moon goddess of Zambia. Bartose and Nalozi women are buried facing west so they can be closer to her in death.

Nyale—Creator of the Bambara people, she gives magical powers to women.

Nyame—Ancient Ashanti earth mother who is the deity of death. She provides a place for her children in her "womb," the earth, when they die.

Oya—Goddess of the Niger River. The personification of the violent rainstorms that formed the river, she can be creative or destructive.

Tsetse—Boshongo goddess of lightning. She brought fire which can be helpful but also can be disastrous. In Togoland, Sodza is the goddess of thunder and her husband is the lightning. Her loud noise drives away evil spirits.

Reclaiming Power—Oshun

Oshun is an African goddess who represents the joy of being female. After fleeing from her father who was jealous of Oshun's popularity with the people, she became the siren of the oceans who saved the lives of sailors. She was eventually reunited with her father who gave her full dominion over the earth's water. The worship of Oshun came over from Africa to Cuba and eventually to America where she is still actively worshipped.

Oshun was a seductress who enjoyed her sexuality and ignored propriety. She delighted in her body and her erotic nature. She loved gold bracelets, silks, and perfumes. She enjoyed seducing males with song, dance, and drums. She was sometimes called mother-whore because she had many husbands and lovers, but she usually had them one at a time. However for all her husband/lovers, Oshun was benefactor, protector, and source of their self-worth. She could not restrict herself to just one husband/lover for very long because she soon became bored. Oshun had many children. She is a goddess of barren women, pregnant women, and women with female problems, such as difficult pregnancies.

Modern Oshuns are women who marry many times, but never look back or feel guilty about moving on. They are the women who always "do it their way" and don't care what others think—the women who are truly feminine, but not necessarily feminine in the ways approved by the current culture. They are the strong, loving, sexual, nurturing, and independent women who love men, but refuse to be possessed or owned by them.

Oshun

African Readings

Asungi. "The Face of Mama is the Blackfaced One." *Women of Power* 15 (Fall/Winter 1990): 36-37.

Brown, Karen McCarthy. "Mama Lola and the Ezilis: Themes of Mothering and Loving in Haitian Vodou." In *Unspoken Worlds: Women's Religious Lives*, edited by Nancy Auer Falk and Rita M. Gross, 235-245. Belmont, CA: Wadsworth Publishing, 1989.

Gillon, Werner. *A Short History of African Art*. New York: Facts on File Publications, 1984.

Gleason, Judith. *Oya: In Praise of the Goddess*. Boston: Shambhala, 1987.

McCall, Daniel, F. "Mother Earth: The Great Goddess of West Africa." In *Mother Worship: Theme and Variations*, edited by James J. Preston, 304-323. Chapel Hill: University of North Carolina Press, 1982.

Murphy, Joseph M. "Oshun the Dance." In *The Book of the Goddess, Past and Present: An Introduction to Her Religion*, edited by Carl Olson, 190-201. New York: Crossroad, 1988.

Paris, Peter J. "From Womanist Thought to Womanist Action." *Journal of Feminist Studies in Religion* 9 (Spring/Fall 1993): 115-126.

Sojourner, Sabrina. "From the House of Yemanja: The Goddess Heritage of Black Women." In *The Politics of Women's Spirituality: Essays on the Rise of Spiritual Power Within the Feminist Movement*, edited by Charlene Spretnak, 57-63. Garden City, NY: Anchor/Doubleday, 1982.

Teish, Luisah. *Jambalaya: The Natural Woman's Book of Personal Charms and Practical Rituals*. San Francisco: Harper & Row, 1985.

Walker, Alice. *The Color Purple*. New York: Harcourt Brace Jovanovich, 1982.

____. *Possessing the Secret of Joy: A Novel*. New York: Harcourt Brace Jovanovich, 1992.

____. *The Temple of My Familiar*. New York: Harcourt Brace Jovanovich, 1989.

Williams, Delores S. "Womanist/Feminist Dialogue: Problems and Possibilities." *Journal of Feminist Studies in Religion* 9 (Spring/Fall 1993): 67-74.

Egypt

Egyptian Goddess History

Egypt's early goddess tradition is evidenced by the many female clay statues discovered from several periods dating between 5500 and 3300 B.C.E. Upper Egypt was then known as the land of the vulture goddess Nekhebt, "Primordial Mother of All Existence," and Lower Egypt as the land of the cobra goddess, Uazit, "Lady of the Night."

Women had a powerful place in ancient Egypt. Property belonged to the women of the family, descent was through the female line, and women and men had equal legal rights. Women's high status was reflected in religion. The primeval goddesses had their own temples in which female priestesses officiated. Queens were the link between one dynasty and the next, as sovereignty descended through the female line as well. Some scholars believe the Egyptian pattern of sister/brother and father/daughter marriages was a way for males to first gain entry into the political power structure. Although several royal couples co-ruled, many Egyptian queens very ably ruled alone, from Mer-Neith in 2800 B.C.E. to Cleopatra in 30 B.C.E. (Seton-Williams, 23-24).

The unification of Egypt and the establishment of a centralized government in 3100 B.C.E. replaced the dual northern and southern capitals with a new capital at Memphis. Nekhebt and Uazit were replaced by new groups of deities in the various cities that developed. The earliest and most authoritative group was that of Heliopolis, which was centered on the worship of Atum, an ancient sun god who was said to have created himself from the "watery waste." Eventually, all the great cities generated their own creation legends and pantheons, where the supreme being was typically a god, his wife, and a male child (Seton-Williams, 25-27).

As the pharaoh came to be thought of as a living god, the supreme goddess was given more subordinate roles. For example, Isis—once revered as the pre-eminent creator and ruler of all of heaven and earth—eventually became a dutiful wife to the god Osiris. The less matriarchal civilization that evolved with the pharaohs, however, was so successful that it remained peaceful and unchanged for some 2,500 years, until Alexander of Rome invaded Egypt in 332 B.C.E. At this time, Greek law was introduced and women began to have an inferior position in society (Seton-Williams, 24). Independent Egyptian history ended with the suicide of the defeated Cleopatra, and the annexation of Egypt into the Roman empire.

However, vestiges of the Great Goddess lingered on. For example, Isis was so popular that she was worshipped for 3000 years, well into the Christian period, throughout the Greco-Roman lands as far north as the Rhine in Germany. In the middle of the sixth century, her chief Egyptian sanctuary was turned into a Christian church. Statues of the dark-skinned Isis at her altars showed her holding the baby Horus; it is thought that she became the inspiration for Mary holding Jesus and that she is one of the many goddesses who evolved into the Black Virgins around the world today (Begg, 13).

Islamic influence continues to suppress the spirit of many Egyptian women today, although there are some positive signs that modern Egyptians may reclaim some of their rich goddess heritage.

Egyptian Goddesses

Ammit — Death goddess with the head of a crocodile, the body of a lion, and the hips and legs of a hippopotamus, she awaits those who die. She devours those who have been evil in life. Also known as the Mistress of the West. Egyptian traditions say that West is where the underworld lies.

Apet — Hippopotamus goddess known as the Goddess of Conception and Birth. She sometimes has a terrifying aspect to frighten away bad spirits. Her talismans aid pregnancy and protect against illness. Other hippopotami goddesses are Nut, Reret, Sheput, and Taueret.

Bast — Sun goddess whose warmth helps the plants to grow. She is also a healer and watches over birth and young children. She is often depicted with a cat's head, an animal highly esteemed by the Egyptians.

Hathor — Sky goddess with the head of a cow and a sun disk resting between her two horns. An independent goddess (an early feminist?), she is the protector of gods and kings. Worshiping her brings fertility, prosperity, and love. As a tree goddess, she incarnates in the sycamore, under which the living and the dead gather to seek her help.

Heqet — Ancient mother goddess who, in the form of a frog, created all beings out of the primordial waters.

Hesat — Divine White Cow. An unguent made of her milk is used to restore the flesh of the deceased. There are many cow goddesses in the Egyptian pantheon.

Isis — Her name translates as "throne" and she is sometimes depicted in that form. She is a savior goddess who has great insight into life and death. She is the goddess from whom all things came.

Kefa — Goddess who gave birth to time. The cosmos revolves around her.

Maat—Protector goddess of justice who breathed life and truth into the first humans. She wears the ostrich feather on her head and carries the scepter and the ankh in her hands.

Mert — The personification of the eighth hour of the night. She manifests as the bark (boat) that carries the shade (spirit of the deceased) through the borderlands of the underworld.

Neith — Ancient goddess whose symbols are the shuttle, bow, and arrow. She is a very complex character, perhaps absorbing aspects of many goddesses. Weaving, hunting, war, and healing are some of her specialities.

Nekhebt — The primordial goddess of Upper Egypt. A creator deity, she also is known for suckling royal children and hovering over the pharaoh in battle.

Sekhmet — Goddess of strength who represents fire and the blasting heat of the sun. She wages war against evil.

Seshat — Stellar and lunar goddess who oversees the written word and is the keeper of architectural knowledge.

Uazit—The primordial goddess of Lower Egypt. She is represented as a cobra and associated with childbirth. When worshipped together, Uazit and her sister Nekhebt are known as Nebit.

Reclaiming Power—Nut

Nut was an Egyptian sky goddess and the wife of the earth god Geb. They clung together, enjoying each other's company while the earth remained in darkness. Their children complained to the god of air about all the darkness. Seeing the need for daylight, he separated them, but promised Nut and Geb that they would be reunited at night.

Nut's body curved over the earth, with her feet in the east and her arms reaching down to touch the earth in the west. The rosy glow of sunrise is said to be her blood from giving birth to the sun each day. As the Mistress of Heaven, she arched her body over the earth and her hair falling down became rain, the source of the rainbow. She swallowed the moon and the stars, and her belly became the starry body of the night.

Nut spent her days working in the sky and Geb spent his days working on the earth—each of them making valuable contributions to the world. Is this the first example of a successful commuting relationship? Nut, separating from her husband in the morning and rejoining him at night, is just one example of the importance of individuals using their unique talents while living their lives in a loving relationship.

Nut is an ancient goddess who shows today's women they can be married and have careers. Women can use their special skills and talents and still have successful relationships. Nut reminds women they can be REAL PARTNERS with their mates.

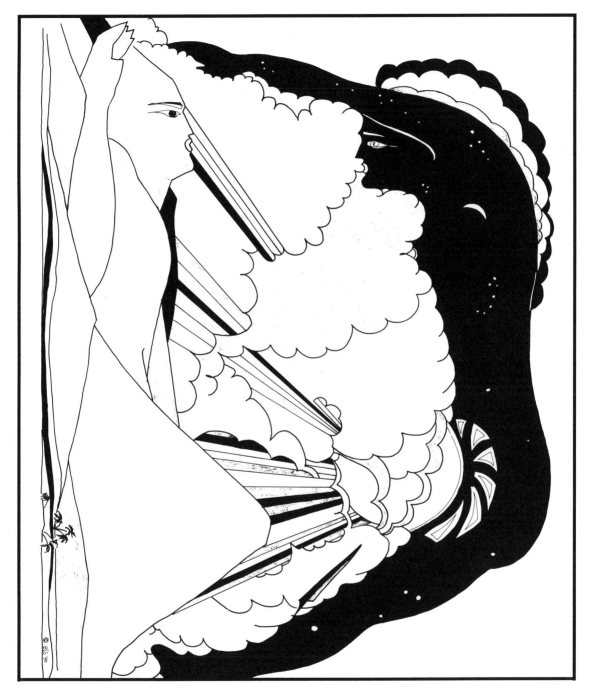

Nut

13

Egyptian Readings

Alexander-Berghorn, Kathleen. "Isis: The Goddess As Healer." In *The Goddess Re-awakening: The Feminine Principle Today*, edited by Shirley Nicholson, 91-99. Wheaton, IL: Theosophical Publishing House, 1989.

Begg, Ean. *The Cult of the Black Virgin*. New York: Aakana/Penguin, 1985.

Betteridge, Anne H. "The Controversial Vows of Urban Muslim Women in Iran." In *Unspoken Worlds: Women's Religious Lives*, edited by Nancy Auer Falk and Rita M. Gross, 102-111. Belmont, CA: Wadsworth Publishing, 1989.

Budge, Wallis E.A. *The Gods of the Egyptians or Studies in Egyptian Mythology*, 203-204. New York: Dover Publications, 1969.

Egan, Rory B. "Isis: Goddess of the 'Oikoumene'." In *Goddesses in Religions and Modern Debate*, edited by Larry W. Hurtado, 123-142. Atlanta: Scholars Press, 1990.

Erman, Adolf. *Life in Ancient Egypt*. New York: Dover, 1971.

Fazzini, Richard A. and William H. Peck. "Excavating the Temple of Mut." *Archaeology* (1983): 16-23.

Freidl, Erika. "Islam and Tribal Women in a Village in Iran." In *Unspoken Worlds: Women's Religious Lives*, edited by Nancy Auer Falk and Rita M. Gross, 125-133. Belmont, CA: Wadsworth Publishing, 1989.

Hoffman, Michael A. *Egypt Before the Pharaohs: The Prehistoric Foundations of Egyptian Civilization*. New York: Alfred A. Knopf, 1979.

James, E.O. *Myth and Ritual in Ancient Near East*. New York: Frederick A. Praeger, 1958.

Kinsley, David. "Isis, Heavenly Queen." In *The Goddesses' Mirror: Visions of the Divine from East and West*, edited by David Kinsley, 165-184. Albany: State University of New York Press, 1989.

McCance, Dawne. "Understandings of 'the Goddess' in Contemporary Feminist Scholarship." In *Goddesses in Religions and Modern Debate*, edited by Larry W. Hurtado, 165-179. Atlanta: Scholars Press, 1990.

Seton-Williams, M.V. "Egypt: Myth and the Reality." In *The Feminist Companion to Mythology*, edited by Carolyne Larrington, 23-47. London: Pandora Press, 1993.

Greece

Greek Goddess History

Inhabited as far back as the Paleolithic era, Greece had continuous settlements during the 3000-year Neolithic period. Small female statuettes of terra cotta and stone have been found from this period, pointing to early goddess worship. The goddess seems to have ruled supreme, since no figure of a god from this period has been found—only statues of male animals.

As the center of trade routes in the Mediterranean, Greece drew religious ideas from many directions, including Phoenicia, Egypt, and Anatolia. The prehistoric (6100-1400 B.C.E.) Cretan religion centered around an earth mother goddess who created and nourished all things (M. Downing, 7-8). The Earth Mother Gaea was seen as divine, animated in water, earthquakes, and molten lava. Her daughters and granddaughters—Themis, Erinyes, the Furies, Demeter, and Persephone—each reflected a different aspect of the earth. Unlike the mainland Greeks, the Minoans of Crete were able to preserve their peaceful goddess religion, uninterrupted by wars for nearly 2000 years, before succumbing to the invading patriarchal Mycenaeans around 1450 B.C.E.

During the period from 1600 B.C.E. to 1150 B.C.E., the Cretan palace at Knossos flourished, representing the full flowering of Neolithic goddess worship, with magnificent frescoes, statues, jewelry, pottery, and architecture. By this time, the goddess had many forms on Crete—goddess of the bee, the birds, the hunt, and the double axe. (The axe is a double-sided symbol of life and death that was used as a ritual tool to sacrifice the bull, the emblem of fertility that renewed the life cycle.) In her many forms, the goddess was worshipped on mountain tops and ocean shores, in palaces and homes.

By 1200 B.C.E., the mainland Mycenaeans were overwhelmed by other patriarchal invaders, the Dorians, bringing the mainland Minoan civilization to an end. The various invading tribes gradually evolved into city-states, each an individual unit ruled by patriarchal leaders. A supreme goddess was a threat to this new god-oriented culture, and revisions to all the Greek myths were rampant. The original goddesses were either inverted to suit the current rulers, or decomposed into many weaker goddesses. Together, the new goddesses made up "the full circle of human qualities. Indeed, each of these arose from the fragmentation of the one goddess, the Great Goddess, the whole female human being who once lived in pre-patriarchal times" (Bolen, xi).

Besides being fragmented, the new Olympian goddesses ... "are not only subordinated to the god, they are defined as related to men and each in a very particular way: Hera is wife, Athena is father's daughter, Aphrodite is the responsive beloved, Artemis shuns men. They are both sentimentalized and denigrated ... and are represented as implacably hostile to one another" (C. Downing, 24).

It is unfortunate that most goddesses known to modern women are from patriarchal Greece. This has given us a false sense of what it is to be a woman—that our identity is in our relationship to a male. Current women are re-envisioning the Greek goddess into the complete and powerful deities they were before patriarchal influence.

Greek Goddesses

Aegle—A nymph famous for her brilliance. Her name means "radiance" and is now used as an art term to describe the brightness of color or light.

Althaea—Mother Earth who nourishes and heals. Having given birth to the sun, she is also responsible for its setting—death.

Aphrodite—Originally a Mediterranean goddess, born from the sea, whom the Greeks absorbed into their religion. She came to be known as a love goddess, representing both carnal and heavenly love. Some think she is hermaphroditic; if so, I think this means that she could find complete love within herself. Burning myrrh and frankincense summons Aphrodite to her worshipers.

Artemis—Goddess of animals. She is one of the oldest Greek deities and may have originally come from Asia Minor. Guardian of all the wild animal kingdom, she protects as well as hunts. As a moon goddess, she oversees weddings and childbirth.

Athena—City goddess often depicted as armed, defending her city. She is a great Olympian deity who has many names, each descriptive of one of her powers. Originally a Minoan or Mycenaean goddess, she is known as the ruler of agriculture, intelligence, vision, health, and domestic crafts. A large temple in her honor remains on the Acropolis in Athens.

Brizo—Goddess of dreams who is worshiped by the women of Delos, a Greek Island. She is also the protector of sailors.

Demeter—Mother goddess who is another of the great Olympian deities with power over the productiveness of the earth and the social order of humans. She is sometimes seen as part of a triad with her daughter Persephone, the youthful one, and Hecate, the elderly one.

Gaea—Primitive mother goddess who came from nothingness. A supreme power, she created everything: the universe, the deities, and humans. From her body, the earth, we are given sustenance.

Hera—Sky goddess with cow-like eyes. Earlier she may have been an earth goddess. Some of the earliest known temples were dedicated to her and she was worshiped long before Zeus. With the advent of patriarchy, she became his wife and lost much of her power.

Muses—Goddesses of the springs who later became responsible for all areas of music and literature. They are generally considered to be a choir of nine: Clio, Calliope, Erato, Euterpe, Melpomene, Polyhymnia, Terpsichore, Thalia, and Urania. Part of the time they live on the Boeotia mountain, Helicon, where there are many springs. It is said that you will become poetic if you drink from the springs.

Persephone—Goddess of the underworld who spends part of her life on the surface of the earth with her mother Demeter. When Persephone is above ground, the plants grow and blossom; she can then return to the underworld with flowers for the dead.

Reclaiming Power—Hectate

Hecate was a Greek goddess, Queen of the Night, Goddess of the Dark Moon, Goddess of Age and Wisdom. Greek women called on her for protection at night. She had magical knowledge and powers and shared these with those who worshiped her. Some worshipers believed she had three heads and could look in three different directions at the same time. She was valued because of her age and wisdom, and shared power as an equal with Zeus for centuries. She was a healer, but because she did not practice in the ways approved by the hierarchy, she was sometimes called a witch. She created and participated in rituals. She was a caretaker of children, flocks, and vineyards.

In a culture that celebrates youth, Hecate reminds us to celebrate the knowing that comes from living beyond childhood, youth, and middle age. She encourages us to leave our old life behind and join her as we age and find peace. She teaches us to honor ourselves as we age by welcoming new energies and power. She wants us to reclaim our magic, our healing ways, to integrate inner powers.

Hecate respects women who continue to be the carriers of culture and tradition AND who want women's traditions and culture reintroduced to the world. We can continue to care for children, but we must find new ways to care for and perhaps find new children. We can continue to care for "flocks," but look for a new definition; we can continue to care for vineyards, but look for the symbolic vineyards that exist in urban areas, inner cities, perhaps even other countries. Finally, Hecate reminds us to consciously remember ourselves as we age and to change; to live as if we really do have three heads. We can look at the past, see the present, and visualize the future. We can change AND LIVE as Hecate did—powerful, wise old women—WOW!

Hecate

19

Greek Readings

Bolen, Jean Shinoda. *Goddesses in Everywoman*. San Francisco: Harper & Row, 1984.

Brindel, June Rachuy. *Phaedra: A Novel of Athens*. New York: St. Martin's Press, 1985.

Burkert, Walter. *Greek Religion*. Cambridge: Harvard University, 1985.

Downing, Christine R. "The Mother Goddess Among the Greeks." In *The Book of the Goddess Past and Present: An Introduction to Her Religion*, edited by Carl Olson, 49-59. New York: Crossroad, 1988.

Downing, Marymay. "Prehistoric Goddesses: The Grecian Challenge." *Journal of Feminist Studies in Religion* (Spring 1985): 7-22.

Goodison, Lucy. *Moving Heaven and Earth: Sexuality, Spirituality and Social Change*. London: Pandora Press, 1992.

Goodrich, Norma Lorre. *Priestesses*. New York: HarperCollins, 1989.

Grigson, Geoffrey. *The Goddess of Love: The Birth, Triumph, Death and Return of Aphrodite*, New York: Stein and Day, 1977.

Keller, Mara Lynn. "The Eleusinian Mysteries of Demeter and Persephone: Fertility, Sexuality, and Rebirth." *Journal of Feminist Studies in Religion* 4, no. 1 (Spring 1988): 27-54.

Kinsley, David. "Athena, Goddess of Culture and Civilization." In *The Goddesses' Mirror: Visions of the Divine from East and West*, edited by David Kinsley, 139-164. Albany: State University of New York Press, 1989.

____. "Golden Aphrodite." In *The Goddesses' Mirror: Visions of the Divine from East and West*, edited by David Kinsley, 185-214. Albany: State University of New York Press, 1989.

Marinatos, Nanno. *Minoan Religion: Ritual, Image and Symbols*. Columbia, SC: University of South Carolina Press, 1993.

Salzman, M. Renee. "Magna Mater: Great Mother of the Roman Empire." In *The Book of the Goddess, Past and Present: An Introduction to Her Religion*, edited by Carl Olson, 60-67. New York: Crossroad, 1988.

Smith, Barbara. "Greece." In *The Feminist Companion to Mythology*, edited by Carolyne Larrington, 65-101. London: HarperCollins, 1992.

Solmsen, Friedrich. *Isis Among the Greeks and Romans*. Cambridge: Harvard University Press, 1979.

Townsend, Joan B. "The Goddess: Fact, Fallacy and Revitalization Movement." In *Goddesses in Religions and Modern Debate*, edited by Larry W. Hurtado, 180-204. Atlanta: Scholars Press, 1990.

India

Indian Goddess History

Goddess worship was prevalent in early India. Sites along a 900-mile stretch of the Indus River, from Harappa to Mohenjodaro, have yielded evidence of an advanced civilization dating back to 3500 B.C.E., a civilization that had a form of writing, large settlements, two-story houses, and religious worship. These sites also contained many elaborate, terra cotta female figurines buried in ritual settings, fashioned in the distinctive Indus Valley style—naked to the waist, often with intricate headdresses, necklaces, bangles, and other ornaments.

Nomadic Aryans conquered the Valley about 2000 B.C.E., displacing the indigenous Indus Valley goddess civilization with their patriarchally-oriented culture and their male gods of war and conquest. The Aryans regarded the native population as dark-skinned inferiors, despite their cultural achievements, and instituted a caste structure that also entailed the subordination of women. The Aryan religion gradually became the religion of the elite.

However, the connection with ancient goddess traditions was maintained in village life, particularly in southern India. Here, female deities continued to be honored up to modern times. For example, the worship of the gramadevata—the local village goddess—persists to this day.

By 1500 C.E., the growth of villages and the spread of the elite religion produced the classical Hindu pantheon. Although the goddess was still seen as a supreme power in her own right, many more subservient goddesses were introduced to explain the subordination of women. Moreover, "There is a duality in mythological Hindu images of the female. The female is seen as the bestower (fertile and benevolent) as well as the destroyer (aggressive and malevolent)" (Abdu-lali, 65). Women are both honored and feared in Indian culture, and the archetype of this duality is the goddess Kali—dreaded and inspiring.

The upbringing of Indian girls today, however, focuses on the subservient goddesses in the Hindu pantheon. A young girl is taught to accept the images of dutiful daughter, sacrificing wife, subservient daughter-in-law, and selfless mother. She learns early to put male needs above her own.

Indian women currently suffer not only gender discrimination, but also caste discrimination, both products of thousands of years of history. Nevertheless, Indian feminists today are trying to unite women by confronting rampant sexist practices: severe limitations in the work place, widespread rape, arranged marriages, female infanticide, unjust divorce laws, sati (widows sacrificing themselves on their husband's funeral pyre), and dowry-deaths. (Dowry-deaths arise when husbands soak their wives in kerosene and burn them because of dissatisfaction with the amount of dowry received from the bride's family.)

Even though there has been little progress in the second-class status of Indian women, there is a glimmer of hope in the resurgent goddess tradition there. Kali's great power and independence can be used as a model for facing and transcending limitations, for liberating women from Indian society's patriarchal bias.

Indian Goddesses

Abhramu-—Hindu goddess known as the "Cloud Knitter." She is a shape changer and the mother of clouds. She was originally a female elephant and the mate of the the god Indra.

Aditi—Nothing existed before this Hindu creator goddess. Coming from the churning ocean, she created everything and protects all. Also known as the Cow of Heaven, she is a fertility goddess overseeing the growth of children and plants. She grants those who worship her their most cherished desire.

Agwani—Hindu fire goddess who is one of the six sisters of Sitala, the goddess of pustular diseases. Agwani causes the fever associated with the diseases.

Annapurna—Food goddess depicted with full breasts that nourish the Hindu inhabitants of Benares. She can be found in homes and upon the mountain named for her. Prayers to her guarantee food.

Apsarases—Celestial goddesses who emerge where there is moisture. These skilled musicians appear as half-human and half-bird; they entertain other deities and the dead.

Devi—Hindu supreme goddess, the ultimate female power who creates, maintains, and destroys. She is a triad, personified in three colors: white, the color of Parvati; red, the color of Durga; and black, the color of Kali. Devi is the amalgam of all Hindu goddesses.

Durga—Warrior goddess who is an aspect of Devi. She is fierce and invincible, and depicted as a beautiful yellow woman with ten arms, sometimes standing on a lion, carrying weapons in each of her ten hands.

Ganga—Water goddess of the Ganges River. She flows from the sky to the underworld, carrying with her those who have died, washing away their sins.

Indrani—Goddess of sexuality who also makes the old young again with the heavenly Kalpa tree (a true "fountain of youth").

Lakshmi—Hindu goddess who has many names. As Bhuti, she is the Goddess of Prosperity; as Sri, she is Mother of the World; and as Hastakamala, she is seen arising out of the primordial ocean holding the lotus, the symbol of good fortune.

Nirriti—Goddess of misery, incarnate as an emaciated elderly black woman. She bears the ill fortune of those born into poverty.

Parvati—Goddess of the Himalayas, a form of Devi. She is the shakti of Shiva, his energizing force. She is sometimes called the Love Goddess. As with other Indian goddesses, she has many names or is merged with other goddesses.

Ratri—Night goddess. She and her sister Usas, the morning goddess, are the Mothers of Heaven. They follow each other across the sky, but their paths never cross.

Shakti—Mother goddess who is the symbol of female energy. It is her energy that animates the gods. A Tantric Hindu goddess who imparts fertility, she is depicted today as a four-armed woman with a child in her lap and a leafy branch in her right hand. Each male god has a female shakti.

Reclaiming Power—Kali

Kali, the Dark Devi, is an Indian goddess who represents fearlessness to women in many countries. She challenges women to accept death, change, and fear of the unknown. By doing so, women can experience the empowerment that comes from overcoming fear. Kali invites women to reclaim and celebrate feminine power and beauty by teaching them to honor their feminine nature, including anger and rage. She encourages the celebration of feminine spirituality, sexuality, fertility, anger, feminine wisdom, and freedom from fear.

In India, worship of Kali is a living tradition. Indian women view the world as unpredictable and threatening, so they seek Kali's protection. Kali's destructive energy can provide strong protection if they stay on her good side. Kali commands great respect because she not only protects them, she helps them conquer their fears.

Western women who are sometimes faced with a threatening, unpredictable world can also use Kali's protection. Perhaps only through conquering our fears can we learn to recognize the creative opportunities in our lives.

The Dark Goddess is present in the many fierce struggles faced by contemporary women. Her mythical presence is felt when a woman faces difficult decisions, breaking through to our unconscious to support us when we take risks. She teaches us to be fearless in overcoming opposition. She is present in our lives, dreams, and creative expressions. Through devotion to Kali, The Fearless, we may reclaim the goddess within, becoming women capable of intimate, loving relationships both with our inner self and with the world outside.

Kali

Indian Readings

Abdulali, Sohaila. "Where Goddesses Walk the Earth: Some Cultural Images of Indian Women." *Woman of Power* (Fall 1986): 65+.

Beyer, Stephan. *The Cult of Tara: Magic and Ritual in Tibet.* Berkeley: University of California, 1978.

Brown, C. Mackenzie. "Kali, the Mad Mother." In *The Book of the Goddess Past and Present*, edited by Carl Olson, 110-123. New York: Crossroad, 1988.

Bumiller, Elisabeth. *May You Be the Mother of a Hundred Sons: A Journey Among the Women of India.* New York: Fawcett Columbine, 1990.

Day, Terence P. "The Twenty-One Taras: Features of a Goddess-Pantheon in Mahayana Buddhism." In *Goddesses in Religions and Modern Debate*, edited by Larry W. Hurtado, 83-122. Atlanta: Scholars Press, 1990.

Fairservis, Walter A., Jr. *The Harappan Civilizations: New Evidence and More Theory.* New York: American Museum of Natural History, 1961.

_____. *The Roots of Ancient India: The Archaeology of Early Indian Civilization.* New York: Macmillan, 1971.

Gross, Rita M. "Hindu Female Deities As a Resource For the Contemporary Rediscovery of the Goddess." In *The Book of the Goddess, Past and Present: An Introduction to Her Religion*, edited by Carl Olson, 217-230. New York: Crossroad, 1988.

Kinsley, David. "Durga, Warrior Goddess and Cosmic Queen." In *The Goddesses' Mirror: Visions of the Divine from East and West*, edited by David Kinsley, 3-24. Albany: State University of New York Press, 1989.

____. "Laksmi, Goddess of Abundance and Luck." In *The Goddesses' Mirror: Visions of the Divine from East and West*, edited by David Kinsley, 53-70. Albany: State University of New York Press, 1989.

Klostermaler, Klaus. "Sakti: Hindu Images and Concepts of the Goddess." In *Goddesses in Religions and Modern Debate*, edited by Larry W. Hurtado, 143-164. Atlanta: Scholars Press, 1990.

Olson, Eleanor. "The Buddhist Female Deities." In *The Goddess Re-awakening: The Feminine Principle Today*, edited by Shirley Nicholson, 80-90. Wheaton, IL: Theosophical Publishing House, 1989.

Preston, James J. *Cult of the Goddess: Social and Religious Change in a Hindu Temple.* Prospect Heights, IL: Waveland Press, 1980.

Teays, Wanda. "The Burning Bride: The Dowry Problem in India." *Journal of Feminist Studies in Religion* 7, no. 2 (Fall 1991): 29-52.

Japan

Japanese Goddess History

The goddess has been worshipped in Japan from the Jomon period, which began about 8,000 B.C.E., up to the present. The many female figurines, believed to be deities, found from the Jomon period are characterized by prominent breasts and pregnant stomachs formed in a complex and distinct "rope-pattern" style.

During the Yayoi period, from 300 B.C.E. to 300 C.E., permanent farming communities and formal tribal organizations evolved into increased social stratification and a more male-dominated religion, but the goddess tradition persisted. In the third century, political consolidation was established under a queen named Pimiko (or Himiko). Her power was apparently based on her shamanistic ability to mediate between the people and the gods (Varley, 5). Shamanism, in fact, has played a significant role in Japan's history, especially in the Ainu culture on the island of Hokkaido.

Another powerful influence is that of the ancient native religion of Japan, Shintoism—"the way of the gods." This religion is based on a benevolent, polytheistic host of deities represented in the forms and forces of nature. In the sixth century, the Tenno clan subdued other clans in Japan and their Shinto goddess, Ama-terasu-o-mi-kami (Amaterasu), was installed as supreme goddess and the national symbol of power. The most venerated shrine in Japan today, the Ise Shrine, is dedicated to this great sun goddess. Amaterasu became the protector of the line of emperors in Japan, a function the current royal family still honors today.

Over time, however, the important role of the goddess was eclipsed. Buddhism was introduced in the sixth century C.E., a religion that initiated sexist privilege for men, patriarchal hierarchies, and androcentric interpretations of key religious texts and concepts (Gross, 65). Japanese feminists say the myths contained in the Kojiki and the Nihongi, which date from around 800 C.E., were written to make sure that gods dominated goddesses and that Amaterasu was intentionally made complementary and conciliatory—the perfect model of the patriarchal woman (Lebra).

Over the centuries, Japanese women gradually lost their autonomy and legal rights as well, increasingly leading secluded lives dominated by their husbands and sons (Lebra). Today, in all the sects throughout the Buddhist world, men still dominate, allowing only a small number of women into leadership positions (Barnes, 131).

Currently, the conservative power in Japanese society continues to emphasize women's capacity for child-bearing and rearing, for perpetuating culture, and for venerating ancestors as their only valid contributions to society. Despite the mythological emphasis on Amaterasu as ancestress of the modern imperial family, Japan still appears to be more male-centered than most industrialized countries.

Japanese Goddesses

Ame-no-uzume-no-mikoto
The large-breasted goddess of mirth, also known as Uzume. She danced before the cave in which Ama-terasu-o-mi-kami hid, helping to draw her out. When Amaterasu emerged, the sun shone again and everyone was joyful.

Askhe-tanne-mat — Ainu spider goddess who appears as a long-fingered woman who helps with childbirth by guiding the newborn out of the birth canal. She is also a war goddess who overcomes male marauders.

Benten — Buddhist goddess shown playing a musical instrument and riding on a dragon, the ancient symbol representing earth and water. She bestows gifts of persuasive speaking, musical talent, and wealth. Anyone desiring an advantageous marriage prays to her on New Year's Day.

Chikisanti — Ainu wood goddess incarnate in the elm tree. She is the mother of the Ainu people, the indigenous, light-skinned inhabitants of Japan. She rules the earth and provides fire.

Chiwash-kor-kami — Ainu water goddess who provides the rain to end droughts. She teaches hunting and fishing rituals to prevent famines (an early enviromentalist?).

Dainichi-nyorai—Buddhist sun goddess who personifies purity and wisdom.

Fuji — Shinto fire goddess who incarnates in the volcano of Mt. Fuji. She spews forth her power and anger in her eruptions.

Hani-yasu-bime-no-kami— Called the "Clay-tempering Princess Deity," she is the patron of potters. In popular belief, she is the goddess of clay and industry.

The Hisa-me — Eight underworld deities who are bogies and frighten children.

Inari — Shinto rice goddess who usually incarnates in a fox. She gives good fortune and long life. She uses fire to forge weapons and is the benefactor of the smiths.

Ishi-kori-dome-no-mikoto Shinto celestial goddess who made the mirror used to entice Ama-terasu-o-mi-kami from her cave.

Izanami-no-kami — Shinto creator goddess who, with her male counterpart, stirred chaos and brought forth the first Japanese island. Together they gave birth to all the Japanese islands and deities.

Kamui Fuchi—Grandmother fire goddess who is the spirit of the hearth in the Ainu home. The fire must be kept burning continuously for it is the entrance to the underworld. She protects from evil and punishes those who do evil.

Kwannon — Buddhist goddess of mercy who delivers all beings from danger. She guides the dead on their path to The Pure Land. In China she is called Guanyin.

Mirume — "Knower of all Secrets." This Buddhist goddess is double-faced, so she can see all secret sins.

Uke-mochi-no-kami—Shinto food goddess who spews food from her mouth for her followers to eat. She is the source of all foods, plant and animal. She is also said to be the provider of silk worms.

Reclaiming Power—Amaterasu

The Japanese sun goddess is an example of a goddess who used her power to end the cruel behavior of her brother, the storm god.

Amaterasu was very angry with her brother's destructive behavior toward the people and told him to stop it, but he ignored her strong objections and continued mistreating the people. She became even more angry when the gods did nothing about her brother's behavior.

She decided to take charge and use her power over light by showing the gods what the world would be like in darkness. She went into a cave, slammed the door, and left the earth dark. The other gods began to worry as rice will not grow in the dark.

The gods, with respect for her authority, punished and banned her brother, but did not know how to let Amaterasu know what they had done. They asked Uzume, goddess of mirth, to sing, dance, and tell jokes outside the cave, hoping Amaterasu would hear the sounds of partying and come out. Amaterasu, hearing the laughter and music, became curious and opened the door of the cave. She immediately saw a large mirror the gods had placed there. She was surprised to see her reflection, and stepped outside to get a better look. The gods immediately slammed shut the door of the cave and light returned to earth. Rice began to grow again.

Amaterasu used her power over light and darkness to right a wrong and to make the earth a safer place for people. Amaterasu's message to women today is that it is okay to have and use power. Power, rather than being used as a means of increasing personal riches, can be used to make a better world.

Amaterasu

Japanese Readings

Barnes, Nancy Schuster. "Buddhism." In *Women in World Religions*, edited by Arvind Sharma, 105-133. Albany: State University of New York Press, 1987.

Brock, Rita Nakashima, Paula M. Cooey, Sheila Greeve Davaney, Rita M. Gross, Anne C. Klein and Rosemary Radford Ruether. "The Questions That Won't Go Away: A Dialogue About Women in Buddhism and Christianity." *Journal of Feminist Studies in Religion* 6, no. 2 (Fall 1990): 87-120.

Chan, Alan K.L. "Goddesses in Chinese Religions." In *Goddesses in Religions and Modern Debate*, edited by Larry W. Hurtado, 9-82. Atlanta: Scholars Press, 1990.

Chen, Ellen Marie. "Tao As the Great Mother and the Influence of Motherly Love in the Shaping of Chinese Philosophy." *History of Religions* 14, no. 1 (August 1974): 51-63.

Durdin-Robertson, Lawrence. *Goddesses of India, Tibet, China and Japan*. Carlow, Ireland: The Nationalist, 1980.

Egami, Namio. *The Beginnings of Japanese Art*. New York: Weatherhill Publishers, 1973.

Gross, Rita M. "Buddhism After Patriarchy?" In *After Patriarchy: Feminist Transformations of the World Religions*, edited by Paula M. Cooly, William R. Eakin, and Jay B. McDaniel, 65-86. Mary Knoll, NY: Orbis Books, 1991.

Kinsley, David. "Amaterasu, the Japanese Ancestral Goddess." In *The Goddesses' Mirror: Visions of the Divine from East and West*, edited by David Kinsley, 71-90. Albany: State University of New York Press, 1989.

Lebra, Joyce, Joy Paulson and Elizabeth Powers. *Women in Changing Japan*. Boulder, CO: Westview, 1976.

Liu, Tao Tao. "Chinese Myths and Legends." In *The Feminist Companion to Mythology*, edited by Carolyne Larrington, 227-250. London: HarperCollins, 1992.

Nakamura, Kyoko Motomochi. "The Significance of Amaterasu in Japanese Religious History." In *The Book of the Goddess, Past and Present: An Introduction to Her Religion*, edited by Carl Olson, 176-189. New York: Crossroad, 1988.

Paper, Jordon. "The Persistence of Female Deities in Patriarchal China." *Journal of Feminist Studies in Religion* 6, no. 1 (Spring 1990): 25-40.

Paul, Diana. "Kuan-Yin: Savior and Savioress in Chinese Pure Land Buddhism." In *The Book of the Goddess, Past and Present: An Introduction to Her Religion*, edited by Carl Olson, 161-175. New York: Crossroad, 1988.

Varley, H. Paul. *Japanese Culture: A Short History*. New York: Praeger Publishers, 1973.

Mesoamerica

Mesoamerican Goddess History

Mesoamerica extends from southern Mexico to Panama, encompassing four distinct cultural areas: the Olmec, Huastec, and Totonac peoples on the Veracruz coast; the Zapotec and Mixtec in the Oaxaca Valley; the Toltec and Aztec in the central basin of Mexico; and the Mayans in the Yucatan peninsula and Guatemala.

Mesoamerican civilizations are very old. Excavations at Zohapilco in Mexico have yielded female figurines dating from 2300 B.C.E. With their bulging hips, these figurines portray "the Mesoamerican vision of the great goddess mother of us all—a mythic image seemingly inevitably associated by planting cultures throughout the world with the fertility of the earth..." (Markman, 32).

Archaeological evidence shows that as tribal life became more directly tied to horticulture, the figurines become finer and more complex, varied, and abundant. Several styles of "pretty ladies" found at ancient sites have been cataloged. One particularly rich source was the prehistoric village of Tlatilco where numerous female figurines were buried alongside women in the cemetery, a site that pointed "to the high status of women in early village cultures" (Markman, 34). Goddess worship also seems to be have been prevalent during these times; in fact, two islands off the coast of the Yucatan Peninsula were used as shrines to the goddess Ixchel.

Over time, the small ceramic "pretty ladies" gave way to the monumental stone sculptures of the Mayan and Aztec civilizations, which lasted from about 2000 B.C.E. to 200 C.E. During this period, attention turned to masculine, complex urban societies rather than maternal forms of household-based cultures. A corresponding change occurred in mythic emphasis from the earth to the heavens, with the new deities revolving around the sun, moon, and stars.

By 1425 the warrior Aztecs dominated the basin of Mexico and, at the time of the Spanish conquest in 1519, controlled most of Mesoamerica. What was left of the indigenous religions was extinguished by the invading Spaniards. The violent changeover to Catholicism is well-documented; lesser known are the more peaceful shifts. For example, in 1531, a remarkable event occurred on the hill of Tepeyac, the hill where the Aztec earth and fertility goddess Tonanitzin once was worshiped. Our Lady of Guadalupe, a manifestation of the Virgin Mary, appeared to a peasant and thus began the transformation of religious life for many natives.

Our Lady of Guadalupe became so popular that an immense shrine was erected on the hill. Today, she represents the national worship of a modern goddess who is "mother, protectress, and preserver of life, health, and happiness, the combined image of Guadalupe/Tonanitzin (which) transforms and binds together the diverse cultural streams of Mexican society..." (Campbell, 13). Yet she is also used to defend a Mexican family life that is reserved for male privilege. In order to resolve that role-model dilemma, modern Mexican religious feminists are re-membering and re-storying ancient goddess tales, such as that of Coyolxauhqui, while seeking a more egalitarian role in society.

Mesoamerican Goddesses

Aiaghom Naum — Wisdom Mother of the Maya, she is the creator of intelligence and is responsible for the incorporeal part of the world.

Centeotl — Maize goddess of the Nahua people of Mexico. She is sometimes shown as a frog in pre-Columbian manuscripts.

Chalchchuitlicue—Aztec water goddess who flows as a slow, meandering stream, nourishing plants or rising as a mist above the land. In larger bodies of water, she becomes the rising and falling waves, or the foam, able to change her color from blue to jade to white.

Chicomecoatl—As the young corn goddess, the Aztecs called her Xilonen and she can be seen as a joyfully dancing maiden with hair like cornsilk. Maturing, her face assumes the colors of corn: yellow, red, purple, or black. Chicomecoatl requires that her corn be planted during the waning moon or it will not grow.

Cihuateotl—Cihuateotl gathers all the spirits of women who die in childbirth. She travels with the sun, searching for lost children. Because she carries the sun as a shield, she is sometimes seen as an Aztec war goddess.

The Cihuateteo — Aztec women who die in childbirth and become deified. They inhabit Cihuatlampa, the place of women in the underworld, and they accompany the sun when it passes through the underworld at night.

Ix Chebel Yax — Daughter of Ixchel who carries in her hand a hank of cotton, teaching weaving and spinning. Incarnate as a spider, she is the greatest Mayan weaver of all.

Ixchel — Mayan moon goddess who protects women in childbirth and sends rain to make the plants grow. She directs the use of plants as medicine and is the giver and taker of life.

Ix Tub Tun — Mayan snake goddess who spits precious stones and rain.

Mayauel — Aztec mother to all people who manifests herself as the milk-laden maguey plant so she will have 400 "breasts" to nurse her children. Her leaves become thatch for houses or cords; her thorns provide pins and needles; her pulp is made into paper; and her cooked root becomes food. (What a benevolent Aztec mother!)

Tonanitzin—"Revered Mother." Aztec mother goddess of earth and corn who is honored at the winter solstice. She became identified with the Virgin (Mary) of Guadalupe. As the Virgin, she continues to be prayed to for fertility, for protection of mothers in childbirth, and for the care of children.

Xiuhtecuhtli—Aztec goddess of fire, she lights the hearth fires for heat and cooking.

Xmucane — Grandmother goddess is older than all other deities. She brings forth the day with light, and fashioned the first Mayan out of finely ground corn flour moistened with water. As generator of all things, she is the divine midwife and predicts the future of newborns. Because she is an incorporeal being, there can be no image of her.

Reclaiming Power—Coyolxuahqui

Coyolxuahqui is an Aztec moon goddess. She is the crescent moon representing a virgin. Her mother was the goddess Coatlicue. One day, when Coatlicue was sweeping out the temple, a feather descended from the air. Coatlicue took the feather and put it next to her bosom. Much to her dismay, she became pregnant. When her sons found out, they were angry and said that her pregnancy was a dishonor to them and decided to kill her.

Coyolxuahqui ran to warn her mother. When her brothers came, they killed their sister in revenge. Coatlicue took her daughter's head and threw it up into the sky, where it became the moon.

This story signaled the end of goddess worship in the Aztec world of Mesoamerica. From this time on, religion became a series of wars and human sacrifices were conducted in religious ceremonies to appease the male Aztec gods. The Aztecs carved a huge, round stone depicting the dismembered body of Coyolxuahqui and placed it at the foot of the temple to remind the people of her faithlessness to her brothers. The Aztecs enacted this story at the Templo Mayor by sacrificing people and throwing their bodies down the temple steps.

Coyolxuahqui is being remembered by modern women of Mexico City today. Ceremonies are held to recreate the goddess within. This story reminds us that going against patriarchy has its risks, that standing up for our mothers and our sisters may result in personal crisis and danger.

Coyolxuahqui

Mesoamerican Readings

Anton, Ferdinand. *Woman in Pre-Columbian America*. New York: Abner Schram Pub., 1973.

Bastide, Roger. *The African Religions of Brazil: Toward a Sociology of the Interpenetration of Civilizations*. Baltimore: Johns Hopkins University, 1978.

Campbell, Ena. "The Virgin of Guadalupe and the Female Self-Image." In *Mother Worship: Theme & Variations*, edited by James J. Preston, 5-24. Chapel Hill: U of North Carolina Press, 1982.

Gonzalez-Wippler, Migene. *Santeria: An African Religion in America*. Boston: Beacon, 1988.

Grovijahn, Jane M. "Grabbing Life Away From Death: Women and Martyrdom in El Salvador." *Journal of Feminist Studies in Religion 7*, no. 2 (Fall 1991): 19-28.

Harvey, Penelope. "South America: The Interpretation of Myth." In *The Feminist Companion to Mythology*, edited by Carolyne Larrington, 388-410. London: HarperCollins, 1992.

Isasi-Diaz, Ada Maria, Elena Olazagasti-Segovia, Sandra Mangual-Rodriguez, Maria Antionetta Berrioztbal, Daisy L. Machado, Lordes Arguelles and Raven-Anne Rivero. "Mujeristas: Who We Are and What We Are About." *Journal of Feminist Studies in Religion* 8, no. 1 (Spring 1992): 105-126.

Isasi-Diaz, Ada Maria and Yolanda Tarango. *Hispanic Women, Prophetic Voice in the Church: Toward a Hispanic Women's Liberation Theology*. San Francisco: Harper & Row, 1988.

Markman, Roberta A. and Peter T. Markman. *The Flayed God: The Mythology of Mesoamerica*. New York: HarperCollins Publishers, 1992.

Nicholson, Henry B. "Religion in Pre-Hispanic Central Mexico." In *Handbook of Middle American Indians*, edited by Robert Wauchope, 395-446. Austin: University of Texas, Vol 10, 1971.

Pasztory, Ester. *Aztec Art*. New York: Harry Abrams Publishing, 1983.

Purkiss, Diane. "Women's Rewriting of Myth." In *The Feminist Companion to Mythology*, edited by Carolyne Larrington, 441-458. London: HarperCollins, 1992.

Rostas, Susanna. "Mexican Mythology." In *The Feminist Companion to Mythology*, edited by Carolyne Larrington, 362-377. London: HarperCollins, 1992.

Thompson, J. Eric S. *Maya History and Religion*. Norman: University of Oklahoma Press, 1970.

Mesopotamia

Mesopotamian Goddess History

Mesopotamia refers to an ancient region that lies between the Tigris and Euphrates Rivers, an area that is now part of Iraq. The southern part of this region is called the "cradle of civilization," with settlements dating back to 4000 or 5000 B.C.E. A remarkable collection of female figurines have been found here from this period, pointing to an ancient goddess cult (James—1959).

Along with the Semitic peoples (see chapter on Semitic-Speaking Peoples), the Sumerians were one of the prominent cultures in Mesopotamia during the Neolithic period. Their religion centered around goddesses and gods of fertility, with death and rebirth in a continuing cycle symbolic of the seasons. The story of the Queen of Heaven and Earth, the Great Goddess Inanna, is recounted on some 5,000 clay tablets that tell of her great popularity and worship. Inanna's descent into the underworld was a metaphor for winter, and her return in the spring signified rebirth. Inanna's return was celebrated in a great fertility festival called Hieros Gamos, the sacred marriage of the king to the goddess (Wolkstein).

The period of goddess worship coincided with a political structure in which women were in charge of all official aspects of Sumerian life. This was a peaceful time, free from invasions of foreign tribes. However, it appears not to have been a time of equality between the sexes, as it seems that kings were sacrificed. Some scholars, such as Dr. Sharon Coggin at Denver's Metro State College, now believe that matriarchy began to collapse on its own before patriarchal tribes invaded Sumeria and then the rest of Mesopotamia. The shift from matriarchy to patriarchy is thought to have evolved between 4000 to 3000 B.C.E., when the kings refused to be sacrificed and used the might of armies to support their claim to the throne.

Other scholars feel that the establishment of animal husbandry around 3000 B.C.E. highlighted the male role in the mystery of procreation, and eventually led to gods gaining power, gradually displacing goddesses altogether (James—1959).

Many invasions from distant peoples and frequent internal shifts in power from one city to another marked the history of Mesopotamia from 3000 to 530 B.C.E. As power shifted between the Sumerians and Semitics, then to the Babylonian Empire, the Assyrian Empire, and the Persian Empire, the conquered peoples assumed the male deities of their conquerors.

As in the ancient tale of the goddess Tiamat, who created horrific creatures to help defend her people but who was eventually slain by the usurpers, one could say that patriarchy killed matriarchy in Mesopotamia and used the body of the goddess to create a new world. Male order was instituted and from the "monster" was created the new patriarchal world order of terrible destruction and violence that exists to this day in Iraq and the Middle East as a whole.

Mesopotamian Goddesses

A—Sumerian moon goddess. Her emblem is a disk from which eight rays emanate. The number eight is associated with goddesses of light in many cultures.

Adamu-—Great mother goddess who produced the first soul from blood. She personifies the blood of childbearing and menstruation and her name means "red."

Aya—Babylonian dawn goddess whose husband was the sun. She gave birth to the world. (Aya is also the name of an African goddess.)

Belit Seri—Known as the "Lady of the Underworld," she keeps records of all human activities. She is often pictured with the goddess Seshat, the scribe who records the deeds of the dead on the Tree of Life.

Damkina—Akkadian earth mother who aids women in childbirth.

Derketo—Chaldean fertility goddess who lives in lakes and has the tail of a fish. Consequently, her followers abstain from eating fish.

Ereshkigal—Sumerian goddess of death, possibly the elder black sister of Inanna. She is the ruler of death and permits the riches of the underworld to return to the earth's surface.

Gestinanna—Sumerian underworld goddess who interprets dreams and is known as a singer and poet. She made a pact in the underworld to secure her brother Dumuzi's release. Now she and her brother divide the year, each spending six months on earth while the other spends six months in the underworld.

Ishtar—Babylonian mother goddess worshiped widely throughout Mesopotamia. Among her many names are Belit, Eshtar, and Tiskhu. Among her many forms are War Goddess, Goddess of Love, Goddess of Fertility and Childbirth, and Goddess of Healing. One story about Ishtar is similar to that of Innana. Ishtar descends to the underworld to see her sister Ereskigal. During her absence the earth is barren, but upon her return from the underworld things begin to grow again.

Mara—Sea goddess who is the Mother of Sumer. As the sea began in darkness, it is into this darkness the night disappears.

Nammu—Sumerian sea goddess who created other deities from the nothing that existed as unformed water.

Ninlil—Ancient Mesopotamian earth goddess known as the Mistress of the Winds. She is the mother goddess of the city of Nippur.

Ninti—Sumerian goddess of healing who may be the basis for the Adam myth. It is said she created children from her ribs.

Pidrai—One of a triad of nature goddess sisters: Pidrai was the light, Tallai was the water, and Arsai was the earth.

Semiramis—Mother goddess and queen of Babylon, famous for her beauty and wisdom. When it was time for her to leave earth, she returned to heaven as a white dove.

Tiamat—Primordial sea goddess who gave birth to all things, both good and evil.

Reclaiming Power—Inanna

The goddess Inanna is Queen of the Above World. She hears a call from the depths (the unknown feminine). Unlike Persephone, who was forced to enter the underworld, Inanna chooses to make the journey. It is important to note that she is in mid-life when she hears the call from the underworld, leading her to a powerful initiation into the mysteries of her unknown self.

Everyone tells Inanna there can be no return—that her trip to the underworld is one way only. But she knows she must make this journey for the sake of her own renewal. She needs to find her own power instead of relying on the power her father gave her. Inanna is not stupid; she knows the risks involved in surrendering male power in order to reclaim female power. She talks to her best friend, Ninshubar, about her plans. She tells Ninshubar if she has not returned within three days to set up a great commotion: alert TV, call newspapers and radio stations, and spread the word that Inanna wants to escape from the underworld.

Inanna starts her journey and as she passes through seven gates, she loses all of her power symbols—her shield, her breastplate, her sword, her jewels, and her clothes—until at the end of the journey she is nude and powerless. Modern women may become powerless if they lose their Gold Card, houses, stocks and bonds, CDs, membership in the health club—all power symbols needed to survive in this culture. Women can lose their power through divorce, widowhood, job loss/discrimination, or disability. All women have gates to pass through just as Inanna did.

Many of us, like Inanna, must find the courage to meet the hidden or confront the unconscious. We too may need a modern Ninshubar to help us escape or to free ourselves from the past. Inanna shows us we can discover our unknown feminine energy, embrace our own inner power, and claim a new life for ourselves and others.

Inanna

Mesopotamian Readings

Barstow, Anne L. "The Prehistoric Goddess." In *The Book of the Goddess, Past and Present: An Introduction to Her Religion*, edited by Carl Olson, 7-15. New York: Crossroad, 1988.

Durdin-Robertson, L. *Goddesses of Chaldea, Syria and Egypt*. Carlow, Ireland: Cesara Publications, 1975.

Ergener, Resit. *Anatolia: Land of Mother Goddess*. Ankara, Turkey: Hitit Publications, 1988.

Gimbutas, Marija. *The Goddesses and Gods of Old Europe: 6500-3500 B.C.* Berkeley and Los Angeles: University of California, 1982.

James, E.O. *Myth and Ritual in the Ancient Near East*. New York: Frederick A. Praeger, 1958.

____. *Prehistoric Religion*. New York: Frederick A. Praeger, 1957.

____. *The Cult of the Mother Goddess: An Archaeological and Documentary Study*. New York: Barnes & Noble, 1959.

Morton, Nelle. "The Goddess As Metaphoric Image." In *The Journey is Home*, edited by Nelle Morton, 147-175. Boston: Beacon, 1985.

O'Brien, Joan and Wilfred Major. In *The Beginning: Creation Myths Form Ancient Mesopotamia, Israel and Greece*. Chico, CA: Scholars Press, 1982.

Ochshorn, Judith. "Ishtar and Her Cult." In *The Book of the Goddess, Past and Present: An Introduction to Her Religion*, edited by Carl Olson, 16-28. New York: Crossroad, 1988.

Pollock, Susan. "Women in a Men's World: Images of Sumerian Women." In *Engendering Archaeology: Women and Prehistory*, edited by Joan M. Gero and Margaret W. Conkey, 366-387. Cambridge, England: Basil Blackwell, 1991.

Wakeman, Mary. "Ancient Sumer and the Women's Movement: The Process of Reaching Behind, Encompassing and Going Beyond." *Journal of Feminist Studies in Religion* 1, no. 2 (Fall 1985): 7-28.

Wolkstein, Diane and Samuel Noah Kramer. *Inanna: Queen of Heaven and Earth*. New York: Harper & Row, 1983.

North America

North American Goddess History

The natives of North America are thought to be descended from northeast Asians who crossed the frozen land bridge near Alaska from 40,000 B.C.E. to 12,000 B.C.E. Native Americans are a diverse group and can be divided into nine geographical areas: the Eskimos in the Arctic; the caribou hunters of the Subarctic areas; the Pacific Northwest Coastal traders and fishers; the peaceful cultures of California; the Southwestern gatherers and herders; the nomadic people of the Great Basin of Nevada and Utah; the shrewd traders of the plateaus; the buffalo hunters of the great plains; the woodland warriors of the Northeast; and the Five Civilized Tribes of the Southeast.

Throughout North America, evidence shows that during both the gathering/hunting and the horticultural periods, the Great Goddess was worshiped as the creator of the earth and all creatures upon it. For example, mother earth statuettes, dating from 1000 B.C.E., have been found in Eastern Woodlands sites. At the Great Indian Mound in Tennessee, a shell was found with a large womb at the center of a design bordered by Spider Woman's emblems.

In most Native American cultures, the goddess is seen as a living being who creates life and takes it away. All forms of life on the planet are seen as her children and therefore all life is sacred. In societies where cultivation of the soil is critical, worship of the earth goddess "is of paramount importance. In many such communities she is the all-powerful divinity. In daily existence her role corresponds to that of woman-mother, the cultivator and keeper of domestic plants and the bearer of children to the world... Undoubt-edly through missionary influence, the Mother Goddess has been suppressed or replaced by a male divinity and the procreative characteristics of the Mother Goddesses have been transferred to the male god" (Hultkrantz, 53-55).

Paula Gunn Allen elaborates on this transfer of power, stating that the belief system of missionaries and other colonizers could not tolerate Native American women occupying decision-making positions. As long as women held such power, the invaders could not persuade the males into subjugating women and adopting their system of male domination. "Since the early 1500s every attempt has been made to replace the gyno-cratic system with the patriarchal system—with such success that no American and few Indian Americans would remember that gynocracy was the primary social order of the Indian America prior to 1800" (Allen, 3).

Unfortunately, this history has made it difficult for contemporary Native American women to appreciate the legacy that is rightfully theirs. As one Tsalagi (Cherokee) native says, "For women to overcome the hypnotism of weakness, of being objects, to overcome the idea that man is either foe or provider, we must stand strong in protecting the earth. We must be alert and not abdicate responsibility and leave it to others. In the brightness of the full moon light and in the quiet of the new moon we make our prayers and medicine that the people can live without fear and have what they need and feel abundance and generosity in their hearts. Getting together and praying in the new and full moon times is a way we can heal ourselves and the earth"(Ywahoo, 9).

North American Goddesses

Aataentsic — Sky goddess known as First Woman of the Iroquois and the Huron peoples. She is worshiped as the dawn or the moon. She is also sometimes considered a malevolent death goddess who cares for the souls of the dead.

A-ha Kachin' Mana—Hopi fertility kachina. Kachina refers to any masked figure among the Pueblo and other southwestern cultures. A kachina can be a meditator spirit between the human and spiritual world; a masked dancer personifying a spirit being; a doll of the spirit; or a spirit of the dead.

Atsentma—Tahltan goddess of meat. Unable to travel because of her pregnancy, she was abandoned by her migrating people. When they left her, she gave birth to all the wild animals that now inhabit the subarctic. Eskimos are careful not to offend her, for if her taboos are broken, she prevents hunters from finding game.

Eastanatlehi — "Changing Woman." Moon Goddess of Eternal Youth, known to both the Navajos and the Apaches. Like the moon, she grows old only to become young again. Turquoise is her earthly symbol.

Cotsipamapot — Omnipotent creator goddess of the Paiute people. When she made humans, she gave them different languages. She is believed to be an ancient woman who is still alive, creating food and giving new life to the dead.

Kokumthena — Shawnee creator goddess who is the most important deity. She made the earth, the sun, the oceans, and humans. Grandmother Kokumthena has gray hair and lives in a grand lodge in the sky.

Loo-wit — One of the five sister mountain goddesses. Loo-wit is the volcano Mt. St. Helens; the others are now known as the mountains Adams, Baker, Hood, and Rainier. The Great Spirit chose Loo-wit to keep her fire lit and easily available to people, reminding them that the Great Spirit is kind.

Memloimis — California water goddess. As water she is formless, yet has form. A malevolent goddess, she attacked creation with a flood.

Sedna — Eskimo Mother of the Sea. Thrown into the ocean by her father, she clung to the side of the kayak. Three times he chopped at her hands to make her let go and the pieces of her hands became the sea animals. She now lives at the bottom of the sea and rules Adliden, the place the dead must go to atone for their sins.

Selu—Cherokee Corn Mother married to the Master of Game. Selu is the provider of maize and beans. The corn goddess is found in many other Native American cultures.

Sussistinnake — "Spider Woman." Creator goddess for many Native American cultures. To the Sia, she was the first being and created two sisters who gave birth to humans. Utset gave birth to Native Americans and Nowutset gave birth to all the others. Spider Woman is responsible for rain, thunder, lightning and the rainbow. It is believed She also saved a piece of the sun so we would have fire on earth. She is sometimes called Spider Grandmother.

Reclaiming Power—Buffalo Woman

Buffalo Woman is a goddess worshiped by many Native Americans. She is an example of a nurturing creation goddess who brings life and food to the people.

Two men were hunting one day when suddenly a beautiful woman appeared in front of them. One saw her, desired her and reached out to possess her. Lightning flashed from the sky and destroyed him. To the other man who treated her with respect she gave a message. He was to tell the people that she was bringing them a holy gift. So he returned, telling the chief that a sacred woman was coming.

Buffalo Woman came bringing the sacred pipe. She taught the people sacred rituals and revealed they were to be a bridge between the sky and earth. She shared the secrets of the holy pipe and how it would help them live a holy way. She spoke to the women compassionately, reminding them that the special gifts from their hands and their bodies were as great as what the warriors did. She spoke to the children, telling them they had a special wisdom and taught them they were not too young to take care of Mother Earth.

She promised to return to every generation to nourish them as they nourish themselves and the earth. As she left, silhouetted against the setting sun, she turned over four times. With each turn she became a different color: black, brown, red, and white. She left the people the buffalo as a source for food, shelter, and clothing.

Modern Buffalo Women are teachers, artists, healers, ministers of all faiths—women who share their special gifts. They are women who reach out to all people, regardless of their gender, race, social or economic status; women who are willing to create nurturing places for others—other families, other communities, or other countries.

Buffalo Woman

49

North American Readings

Allen, Paula Gunn. *Grandmothers of the Light: A Medicine Woman's Sourcebook*. Boston: Beacon Press, 1991.

Allen, Paula Gunn. *The Sacred Hoop: Recovering the Feminine in American Indian Traditions*. Boston: Beacon, 1986.

Cameron, Anne. *Daughters of Copper Woman*. Vancouver, BC: Press Gang, 1981.

____. *Dzelarhons: Myths of the Northwest Coast*. Madeira Park, BC: Harbour, 1986.

Gill, Sam D. and Irene F. Sullivan. *Dictionary of Native American Mythology*. Santa Barbara, CA: ABC Clio, 1992.

Guiley, Rosemary Ellen. "Witchcraft As Goddess Worship." In *The Feminist Companion to Mythology*, edited by Carolyne Larrington, 411-424. London: HarperCollins, 1992.

Hatt, Gudmund. "The Corn Mother in America and in Indonesia." *Anthropos* 46 (1951): 853-914.

Hultzkrantz, Ake. *The Religions of the American Indians*. Berkeley: University of California-Berkeley Press, 1979.

Montreal Museum of Fine Arts. *The Inuit Sea Goddess*. Montreal: Montreal Museum of Fine Arts, 1986.

Moon, Sheila. *Changing Woman and Her Sister*. San Francisco: Guild for Psychological Studies, 1984.

Sonne, Brigitte. "Mythology of the Eskimos." In *The Feminist Companion to Mythology*, edited by Carolyne Larrington. London: HarperCollins, 1992.

Tsing, Anna Lowenhaupt. "The Vision of a Woman Shaman." In *Feminist Research Methods: Exemplary Readings in the Social Sciences*, edited by Joyce McCarl Nielsen, 147-173. Boulder, CO: Westview, 1990.

Tyler, Hamilton. *Pueblo Gods and Myths*. Norman: University of Oklahoma, 1964.

Weigle, Marta. "Southwest Native American Mythology." In *The Feminist Companion to Mythology*, edited by Carolyne Larrington, 333-361. London: HarperCollins, 1992.

Ywahoo, Dhyani. "Woman's Role in Planetary Transformation." *Women of Power* 1 (Spring 1984): 4-9.

Zak, Nancy C. "Sacred and Legendary Women of Native North America." In *The Goddess Re-awakening: The Feminine Principle Today*, edited by Shirley Nicholson. Wheaton, IL: Theosophical Publishing House, 1989.

Semitic-Speaking Peoples

Semitic Goddess History

Dating back to around 8000 B.C.E., Jericho is believed to be the oldest walled and defended town in the world. Two small mother goddess figures found from this period near the Jordan River are typical of many figures found later in neighboring cultures—flowing-gowned females with their hands cupped beneath their breasts.

Along with the Sumerians (see Mesopotamia chapter), the Semites were one of the prominent cultures around 3000 B.C.E. Living in an area that is now known as Syria, Jordan, Israel, Lebanon, and Arabia, the Semites consisted of many peoples, including the Accadians, Canaanites, Arameans, and Arabians. The Canaanite fertility goddess Asherah (a form of the Babylonian goddess Ishtar, herself a version of the original Sumerian goddess Inanna) was part of popular Israelite religion. Her worship was widespread and persisted until the seventh century (Patai, 29-52).

This ancient fertility-based religion, however, came under merciless attack by Josiah, a patriarch who tried to impose monotheism on the polytheistic Canaanites. The attack included slaughtering ritual prostitutes and razing the goddess symbols in temples. Eventually, the peaceful goddess was changed into one of war to coincide with the new patriarchal gods of destruction, as exemplified by the Ugaritic deity Anat, Goddess of Fertility and War (Biale, 240-256).

But the Great Goddess could not be obliterated. Subsequent female figures in Jewish religion were Hokhma, who was merged with Sophia into the personification of wisdom, and Shekhinah, who later came to denote the feminine qualities of a male god.

The Hebrew Bible has given Lilith, Eve, and Mary as models of feminine behavior: one a demon, one a temptress, and one a virgin mother. All are incomplete and impossible models for women today. "Contemporary Jewish feminists are now working on bringing forth our own images of the divine and turning to the creation of new forms to nourish those who are ready for change. In this process, the Shekhinah that is emerging, especially in North America, is a varied Goddess, indeed a Goddess with a thousand faces" (Novick, 45).

Today's Judeo-Christian women are realizing we are more than the sum of Lilith, Eve, and Mary. By doing so, we are learning to recognize our own inner power and to realize that our power can change the world into a more loving and livable place for all human beings.

Semitic Goddesses

Adamah — Earth goddess who receives the dead. In the Hebrew scriptures, she "opened her mouth to receive Abel."

Aholibah — Goddess of Jerusalem who appears sometimes as a woman and sometimes as a mare.

Aimah — Mother goddess who contained within herself the sun, the moon, and the stars. Her story is similar to that of the Egyptian goddess Maut.

Aluka — Goddess of the underworld who had two daughters, Life and Death. She is identical to the Mesopotamian goddess Ereshkigal.

Ama — Mother goddess and creator of all things.

Asherah — Ugarit sea goddess and mother of seventy deities, known for her great wisdom. She demonstrated great love for her son Ba'al by making the bricks for his temple.

Ashtart—Goddess of Heaven who fell as a fiery star into the lake at the sacred shrine of Aphaca. Her early shrines on Cyprus later became shrines to Aphrodite. Ashtart and Ishtar are probably the same goddess, as their stories are very similar and both have a son named Tammuz.

Beth-aven — Golden Calf Goddess worshiped by the Israelites in Sinai. She is probably connected to the Egyptian goddess Hathor and is sometimes called Hegloth.

Binah — Dark Heavenly Mother referred to in the Proverbs. She is an understanding teacher who gives happiness and security to her students.

Eve — First Woman of the Old Testament who was the mother of all living things. She is also known as Chavah.

Hokhma—Goddess of Wisdom who instructs those who seek her out. Perhaps she is the Holy Spirit who is described by some as the female life-giving spirit, the beginning of all. Another spelling of her name is Chokmah.

Husbishag — Semitic underworld goddess who keeps the records which tell the time of our deaths. She is connected to Ereshkigal.

Kades — Goddess of love and sexuality.

Kimah — Celestial goddess who represents the seven stars of the Pleiades.

Mama — Sumerian mother goddess and Semitic fertility deity. She presides over childbirth. Mama gave humans a temporary body and an immortal soul.

Meni — Love goddess who was probably worshiped by Jews in Babylon.

Phlox — Mother of Light, Goddess of Fire. She is the embodiment of the elements.

Shekhinah — Symbol of divine power who is the ocean, the tree of life, and the first light.

Sophia — Mother goddess of all, she is the female form of the holy spirit. As mother of the soul and the mind, she is responsible for the formation and control of wisdom. She is also known by the name Barbelo.

Reclaiming Power—Lilith and Eve

In the beginning, according to the first creation story in the Bible, a male and a female were created in the image of God. God instructed them to "have dominion over the earth and all its inhabitants." An eleventh century Cabbalistic document, *The Alphabet of Ben Sira*, says these first people were Adam and Lilith.

Lilith tried to live with Adam sharing everything equally. Adam, however, wanted to be the one in charge, and ordered Lilith to wait on him and do all the everyday chores. Finally, Lilith told Adam that if living in the garden meant doing everything Adam's way, she was leaving, and she did!

Adam didn't like being alone and having all the responsibility for the garden with no help. He went to God and asked for a new woman, one who would know her place in the garden and who would do things Adam's way. God hypnotized Adam and took one of his ribs and made Eve. Now Eve liked being in the garden, even as an assistant, but sometimes she knew her ideas made more sense than Adam's. Also, there were times when she wished she had someone to talk to just like Adam talked to God.

Adam told Eve about the "other woman" Lilith, who used to live in the garden. One time, after Lilith had tried unsuccessfully to return to the garden, Eve climbed over the wall to meet her. They began talking and Eve discovered that in the beginning God made man and woman equal, not one ruling over the other. They talked of many things, they laughed and cried together, and a bond of sisterhood grew between them.

This patriarchal Biblical myth is one of many that discourages female bonding. It is time for women to look at the "stories" told about them. It is time to ask why only the "Adams" of the world decide how things are done and why "Adam's" way is not only the best way—but the only way. IT IS ALSO TIME TO CELEBRATE WOMEN'S FRIENDSHIPS!

54

Lilith and Eve

Semitic Readings

Ashe, Geoffrey. *The Virgin Mary's Cult and the Re-Emergence of the Goddess.* New York: Arkana Paperbacks, 1976.

Baile, David. "The God with Breasts: El Shaddai in the Bible." *History of Religions* (February 1982): 240-256.

Begg, Ean. *The Cult of the Black Virgin.* New York: Aakana/Penguin, 1985.

Berger, Pamela. *The Goddess Obscured: Transformation of the Grain Protectress From Goddess to Saint.* Boston: Beacon, 1985.

Davies, Steve. "The Canaanite-Hebrew Goddess." In *The Book of the Goddess, Past and Present: An Introduction to Her Religion,* edited by Carl Olson, 68-79. New York: Crossroad, 1988.

Frymer-Kensky, Tikva. *In The Wake of the Goddesses: Women, Culture, and the Biblical Transformation of Pagan Myth.* New York: Free Press/Macmillan, 1992.

Koltuv, Barbara Black. *The Book of Lilith.* York Beach, ME: Nicolas-Hays, 1984.

Mascetti, Manuela Dunn. *The Song of Eve.* New York: Fireside/Simon & Schuster, 1990.

Matthews, Caitlin. *Sophia: Goddess of Wisdom—The Divine Feminine From Black Goddess to World Soul.* New York: Mandala/HarperCollins, 1991.

Neudel, Marian Henriquez. "Innovation and Tradition in a Contemporary Midwestern Jewish Congregation." In *Unspoken Worlds: Women's Religious Lives,* edited by Nancy Auer Falk and Rita M. Gross, 179-188. Belmont, CA: Wadsworth Publishing, 1989.

Novick, Rabbi Leah. "Encountering the Shekhinah." *Women of Power* 15 (Fall/Winter 1990): 45-47.

Pagels, Elaine. *Adam, Eve, and the Serpent.* New York: Vintage, 1989.

Patai, Raphael. *The Hebrew Goddess.* New York: Avon Books, 1978.

Siegele-Wenschkewitz, Lenore, Judith Plaskow, Marie-Theres Wacker, Fokkelein van Dijk-Hemmes, and Asphodel P. Long. "Feminist Anti-Judaism." *Journal of Feminist Studies in Religion* 7, no. 2 (Fall 1991): 95-132.

Warner, Marina. *Alone of All Her Sex: The Myth and the Cult of the Virgin Mary.* New York: Vintage, 1978.

Further Readings

Adler, Margot. *Drawing Down the Moon*. Boston: Beacon Press, 1979.

Anderson, Sherry Ruth and Patricia Hopkins. *The Feminine Face of God: The Unfolding of the Sacred in Women*. New York: Bantam, 1991.

Ann, Martha and Dorothy Imel. *Goddesses in World Mythology*. Santa Barbara, CA: ABC-CLIO, 1993.

Austin, Hallie Inglehart. *The Heart of the Goddess*. Berkeley: Wingbow, 1990.

Baring, Anne and Jules Cashford. *Myth of the Goddess: Evolution of An Image*. London: Viking Arkana, 1991.

Belenky, Mary Field, Blythe McVicker Clinchy, Nancy Rule Goldberger and Jill Mattuck Tarule. *Women's Ways of Knowing: The Development of Self, Voice, and Mind*. New York: Basic Books, 1986.

Bell, Diane. *Daughters of the Dreaming*. North Sydney, Australia: McPhee Gribble, 1983.

Binford, Sally R., Merlin Stone, Charlene Spretnak and Sally R. Binford. "Are Goddesses and Matriarchies Merely Figments of Feminist Imagination?" In *The Politics of Women's Spirituality: Essays on the Rise of Spiritual Power Within the Feminist Movement*, edited by Charlene Spretnak, 541-562. Garden City, NY: Anchor/Doubleday, 1982.

Bradley, Marion Zimmer. *Mists of Avalon*. New York: Pocket Books, 1988.

Campbell, Joseph, editor. *In All Her Names: Explorations of the Feminine in Divinity*. San Francisco: Harper & Row, 1991.

Canan, Janine. *She Rises Like the Sun: Invocations of the Goddess*. Freedom, CA: Crossing Press, 1989.

Christ, Carol P. "Why Women Need the Goddess: Phenomenological, Psychological, and Political Reflections." In *Laughter of Aphrodite*, edited by Carol P. Christ, 273-287. San Francisco: Harper & Row, 1987.

Christ, Carol P. and Judith Plaskow. *Womanspirit Rising: A Feminist Reader in Religion*. New York: Harper & Row, 1979.

Condren, Mary. *The Serpent and the Goddess: Women, Religion, and Power in Celtic Ireland*. San Francisco: Harper & Row, 1989.

Cooey, Paula M. et al. *After Patriarchy: Feminist Transformations of the World Religions*. New York: Orbis Books, 1991

Daly, Mary. *Gyn/Ecology: The Metaethics of Radical Feminism*. Boston: Beacon, 1978.

Dames, Michael. *The Silbury Treasure: The Great Goddess Rediscovered*. London: Thames and Hudson, 1979.

Dexter, Miriam Robbins. *Whence the Goddesses: A Source Book*. New York: Pergamon, 1990.

Durdin-Robertson, Lawrence. *The Year of the Goddess: A Perpetual Calendar of Festivals*. Wellingborough, Northamptonshire, England: Aquarian Press, 1990.

Ehrenberg, Margaret. *Women in Prehistory*. Norman: University of Oklahoma Press, 1989.

Eisler, Riane. *The Chalice and the Blade: Our History, Our Future*. San Francisco: Harper & Row, 1987.

Eisler, Riane and David Loye. *The Partnership Way. New Tools for Living and Learning, and Healing Our Families, Our Communities and Our World*. San Francisco: Harper & Row, 1990.

Gadon, Elinor W. *The Once & Future Goddess: A Sweeping Visual Chronicle of the Sacred Female and Her Reemergence in the Cultural Mythology of Our Time*. San Francisco: Harper & Row, 1989.

Galland, China. *Longing for Darkness: Tara and the Black Madonna*. New York: Penguin, 1990.

Gimbutas, Marija. *The Language of the Goddess*. San Francisco: Harper & Row, 1989.

_____. *The Civilization of the Goddess. The World of Old Europe*. San Francisco: Harper & Row, 1991.

Hubbs, Joanna. *Mother Russia*. Bloomington: Indiana University Press, 1988.

Hultkrantz, Ake. *The Book of the Goddesses*. New York: Crossroad Publishing, 1983.

Inglehart-Austen, Hallie. *The Heart of the Goddess: Art, Myth, and Meditations of the World's Sacred Feminine*. Berkeley: Wingbow Press, 1990.

Johnson, Buffie. *The Lady of the Beasts*. San Francisco: Harper & Row, 1989.

Larrington, Carolyne. *The Feminist Companion to Mythology*. London: Pandora/HarperCollins, 1992.

Lerner, Gerda. *The Creation of Patriarchy*. New York: Oxford University Press, 1986.

Monaghan, Patricia. *The Book of Goddesses and Heroines*. New York: Dutton, 1981.

Morgan, Robin, Merlin Stone, Gloria Steinem, Siew Hwa Beh, Margot Adler, Bella Debrida, and Judy Chicago. "Mythic Heros As Models of Strength and Wisdom." In *The Politics of Women's Spirituality: Essays on the Rise of Spiritual Power Within the Feminist Movement*, edited by Charlene Spretnak, 87-158. Garden City, NY: Anchor/Doubleday, 1982.

Nicholson, Shirley. *The Goddess Re-Awakening: The Feminine Principle Today*. Wheaton, IL: Theosophical Publishing House, 1989.

Nobel, Vicki, editor. *Uncoiling the Snake: Ancient Patterns in Contemporary Women's Lives*. San Francisco: Harper & Row, 1993.

O'Flaherty, Wendy Doniger. *Women, Androgynes, and Other Mythical Beasts*. Chicago: University of Chicago Press, 1980.

Orenstein, Gloria Feman. *The Reflowering of the Goddess*. New York: Pergamon Press, 1990.

Perera, Sylvia Brinton. *Descent to the Goddess*. Toronto: Inner City Books, 1981.

Phillips, John A. *Eve: The History of an Idea*. San Francisco: Harper & Row, 1984.

Plaskow, Judith and Carol P. Christ, editors. *Weaving the Visions*. San Francisco: Harper & Row, 1989.

Preston, James J. , editor. *Mother Worship: Theme & Variations*. Chapel Hill: U of North Carolina Press, 1982.

Ruether, Rosemary Radford. *Womanguides*. Boston: Beacon Press, 1985.

____. *Sexism and God-Talk: Toward a Feminist Theology*. Boston: Beacon, 1983.

Rufus, Anneli S. and Kristan Lawson. *Goddess Sites: Europe*. San Francisco: HarperCollins, 1991.

Sharma, Arvind, editor. *Women in World Religions*. Albany: State University of New York Press, 1987.

Sharma, Arvind and Katherine K. Young. *The Annual Review of Women in World Religions*, Vol. 1. Albany: State University of New York Press, 1991.

Sjoo, Monica and Barbara Mor. *The Great Cosmic Mother: Rediscovering the Religion of the Earth*. San Francisco: Harper & Row, 1987.

Starhawk. *The Spiral Dance: A Rebirth of the Ancient Religion of the Great Goddess*. San Francisco: Harper & Row, 1979.

____. *Truth Or Dare: Encounters With Power, Authority, and Mystery*. San Francisco: Harper & Row, 1976.

Stein, Diane. *The Women's Spirituality Book*. St. Paul: Llewellyn, 1987.

Stone, Merlin. *Ancient Mirrors of Womanhood*. Boston: Beacon Press, 1979.

____. *When God Was A Woman*. New York: Harvest/HBJ, 1976.

Spretnak, Charlene, editor. *The Politics of Women's Spirituality: Essays on the Rise of Spiritual Power Within the Feminist Movement*. Garden City, NY: Anchor/Doubleday, 1982.

Tong, Rosemarie. *Feminist Thought: A Comprehensive Introduction*. Boulder, CO: Westview, 1989.

Walker, Barbara. *Woman's Encyclopedia of Myths and Secrets*. San Francisco: Harper & Row, 1983.

Young, Serinity, editor. *An Anthology of Sacred Texts By and About Women*. New York: Crossroad, 1993.

Whitmont, Edward. *The Return of the Goddess*. New York: Crossroad, 1986.

Wynne, Patrice. *Womanspirit Sourcebook*. San Francisco: Harper & Row, 1988.

ISBN #0-9638567-0-7

$9.95